6.1
1.0

Life Skills

Change

Making the Best of It

by Robert Wandberg, PhD

Consultants:
Roberta Brack Kaufman, EdD
Dean, College of Education
Concordia University
St. Paul, Minnesota

Millie Shepich, MPH, CHES
Health Educator and District Health Coordinator
Waubonsie Valley High School
Aurora, Illinois

LifeMatters
an imprint of Capstone Press
Mankato, Minnesota

Thank you to Heather Thomson of BRAVO Middle School, Bloomington, Minnesota; to Christine Ramsay of Kennedy High School, Bloomington, Minnesota; and especially to all of their students, who developed the self-assessments and provided many real stories.

LifeMatters Books are published by Capstone Press
PO Box 669 • 151 Good Counsel Drive • Mankato, Minnesota 56002
http://www.capstone-press.com

Printed in the United States of America

Library of Congress Cataloging-in-Publication Data
Wandberg, Robert.
      Change: Making the best of it / by Robert Wandberg.
            p.   cm. — (Life skills)
      Includes bibliographical references and index.
      ISBN 0-7368-0700-4 (hardcover) — ISBN 0-7368-8841-1 (softcover)
      1. Teenagers—Life skills guides—Juvenile literature. 2. Life change events—Juvenile literature.
I. Title.
      HQ796 .W242 2000
      646.7´00835—dc21   00-037070
                                                    CIP

Summary: Describes what change is, and how it affects teens. Suggests ways to deal with change, including several self-assessments to help teens judge how well they cope with change.

Staff Credits
Charles Pederson, editor; Adam Lazar, designer; Katy Kudela, photo researcher

Photo Credits
Cover: UPmagazine/©Tim Yoon
©Artville/Don Carstens, 21
Index Stock Photography, 57
International Stock/©Jay Thomas, 7; ©James Davis, 59
PNI/©DigitalVision, 13
©StockByte, 26, 47
Unicorn Stock Photos/©Karen Holsinger Mullen, 51; ©Tom McCarthy, 55
Uniphoto, 29/©Robert Sherbow, 8; ©Caroline Woodham, 33; ©Jim Olive, 37; ©Kent Knudson, 43
UPmagazine/©Tim Yoon, 5, 15, 25, 35, 45, 53

A 0 9 8 7 6 5 4 3 2 1

Table of Contents

Chapter Overview

Everything changes. Change can be either negative or positive.

It's not always easy to decide if a change is good or bad. Two people may see the same change in different ways.

A self-assessment can help you understand what you think about change.

CHAPTER 1

Change: ☼
You Can't Run,
You Can't Hide

Every day, life changes. Events, your surroundings, emotions, and people play a larger or smaller role in your life than they did before. You can identify and handle change in healthy, productive ways. In this chapter you will begin to understand **ChangeMatters.**

DID YOU KNOW?

In 1885, the first successful gasoline-driven car reached a speed of 9 miles per hour at Mannheim, Germany.

Change All Around

We have entered a new century and millennium. Many things have changed completely. For example, in the entire year of 1900, 36 people died in car crashes in the United States. Today we average about 42,000 car fatalities in the U.S. each year. Life expectancy of Americans in 1900 was about 47 years. A U.S. citizen born in 1998 can expect to live 77 years. Canadian life expectancy has reached 79 years. In 1900, 3 million people in the United States were 65 or older. Today about 34 million are over that age.

The world changes constantly. We don't even notice many of those changes. The trees around us grow taller. Their leaves turn from green to beautiful shades of yellow, orange, and brown.

How have you changed? Most of your changes have probably been positive. You may be taller, stronger, and more independent. You have gained many skills in reading, writing, and math. You make important decisions and communicate thoughts and feelings.

Positive and Negative Change

Change happens in many areas. As you read through this list, you might think only of negative changes. Imagine how these areas could bring positive changes.

- School or work routines

- Our health or that of people we know

- Time we spend in personal routines or commitments

- Our personality, attitudes, or feelings toward ourselves and others

- Our physical or social environment, which include things and people around us

- How much money we have

- Future goals and dreams

- Relationships with other people

Positive change can improve our well-being. It can improve our self-esteem, confidence, social life, and relationships. Change also can be positive when we remove some negative situations.

Dealing with positive change is often but not always more comfortable than dealing with negative change. For example, it may be positive that you make more money at your job. However, you also may have more difficult responsibilities.

Sometimes, one person sees a change as negative, and another person sees it as positive. Suppose someone you knew was laid off from a job and replaced by a robot. That person would likely view the change as negative. However, the president of the company might view the change as positive.

Change can be gradual. For example, you can't watch your fingernails grow. Some changes happen without warning. An example might be the divorce of two people that creates an unanticipated shock for their child.

DID YOU KNOW?

The Amish people of the eastern and midwestern United States and Ontario, Canada, are known for resisting change. The Amish wear plain, homemade clothing, farm their land using horse-drawn machinery, and live in homes without electricity. As a rule, the Amish do not have telephones in their homes and reject most forms of technology.

Finn, Age 15

When Finn's parents divorced, he thought the knot in his stomach would never go away. He was mad that his parents were messing up his life. He was scared he'd have to change schools. He was nervous about what his friends would think. He wondered how he'd feel about living with his mother. How would it be to see his dad one evening a week and every other weekend?

A year later, Finn says, "My life is different, but it's not bad. My parents fought all the time, and things are a lot quieter around the house since they split. They're both happier and more fun to be with. Some people just shouldn't live together. I thought people would treat me differently, but they didn't. A lot of kids go through a big change like this. It was hard, but you can usually find something good in it. I'm actually seeing my dad more now than when we all lived together."

When negative change happens, we may have some good ideas on how to make things better. Knowing what do to is the first step. Putting that knowledge into action is what really counts. The best plans and ideas are useless unless they are put into action.

FAST FACT

Communications is one of the fastest changing industries. For example, telephones have been basic necessities in most North American homes for years. However, the wireless phone industry is fairly new, starting about 25 years ago. In 2000, 87 million people in the United States had wireless phones. By the time you read this, the number will be much higher. Ask those people if they could live without their cell phones, and they'd probably say no!

Examples of Change

It is often difficult to judge what effect germs might have on a person. A germ may cause one person to become ill, whereas another person may be resistant to it. This difference in resistance could be the result of heredity, age, physical condition, or a combination. Likewise, it is often difficult to judge what effect change might or might not have on a person.

Look at these situations. Is the change positive or negative?

Deena's mother remarries.

Vinnie's family inherits a lot of money.

Pang's family moves to a newer home.

Andrew has a new baby sister.

A new classmate sits next to Melissa.

Chris's neighbor moves to a new town.

Hillary transfers to a different school.

Olivia's grandmother moves to a nursing home.

Daniel loses 30 pounds.

Change

At first glance, these life changes may seem clearly positive or negative. However, as you consider the possibilities more deeply, the answer may be less clear. For example, is losing 30 pounds positive or negative? If Daniel lost 30 pounds in a medically safe manner, his health may improve. The weight loss would result in a reduced risk for many health problems. However, if Daniel lost weight in medically dangerous ways, it might increase his health risks.

Self-Assessments and Change

Self-assessments are tests that can give you information to help you know yourself better. There are many kinds of self-assessments. Teen self-assessments often are about relationships. You can learn a lot about your health from some self-assessments. Common topics include risk of heart disease, cancer, or mental illness. Other topics may include attitudes toward the death penalty or abortion, which ends a pregnancy early. Schools may provide self-assessments to help students choose the right career.

Periodically assessing yourself can help you keep track of what is normal for you. The key to self-assessments is that *you* interpret the information, not someone else.

Self-assessments also can help us determine how we have changed. Teens developed the following self-assessment. It shows what they consider important to think about in handling change.

Read items 1–15 below. For each item, choose the number following it that best describes you. Write it on a sheet of paper. Use this rating scale:

1 = Never	2 = Sometimes		3 = Always	
1. I eat a balanced diet.	1	2	3	
2. I avoid using tobacco, alcohol, or other drugs.	1	2	3	
3. I get enough sleep.	1	2	3	
4. I feel I am worth something.	1	2	3	
5. I recognize change and stress.	1	2	3	
6. I have a good sense of humor.	1	2	3	
7. I manage my time effectively.	1	2	3	
8. I handle my emotions effectively.	1	2	3	
9. I exercise to handle my emotions.	1	2	3	
10. I know how and when to relax.	1	2	3	
11. I am optimistic.	1	2	3	
12. I am a member of an organized team, club, or group.	1	2	3	
13. I put my goals in the order of their importance.	1	2	3	
14. I can view change as good instead of bad.	1	2	3	
15. I know where to get professional help if necessary.	1	2	3	

Add up your points. The closer your point total is to 45, the better you can handle change. You might have scored 1 or 2 on some items. That just shows you where you need some practice.

Points to Consider: ChangeMatters

Can change be both positive and negative? Explain.

Give some examples of change in your life that you might not always notice.

Choose two items from the self-assessment on which you could improve. How could you improve?

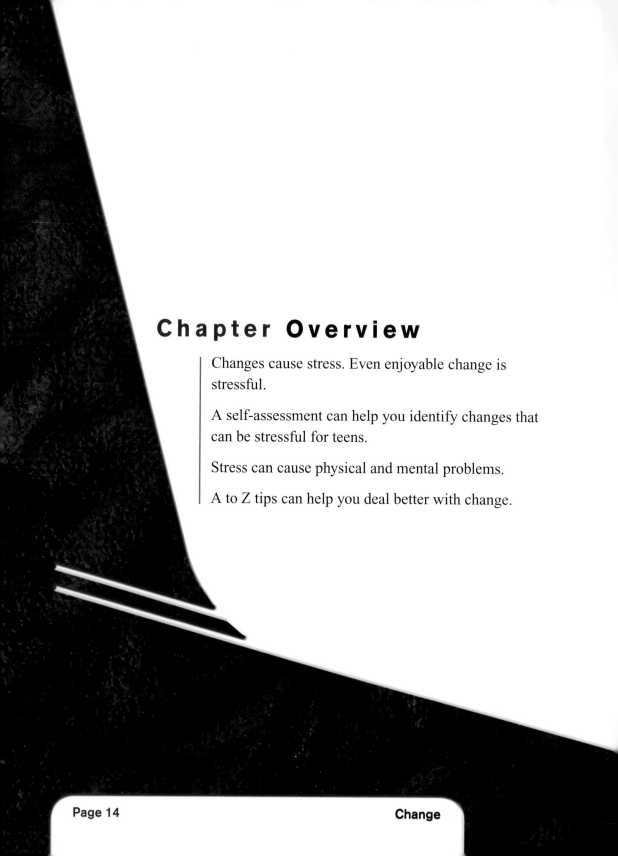

Chapter Overview

Changes cause stress. Even enjoyable change is stressful.

A self-assessment can help you identify changes that can be stressful for teens.

Stress can cause physical and mental problems.

A to Z tips can help you deal better with change.

Change

CHAPTER 2

Changes, Challenges, and Stresses

Change causes stress, which affects our behavior, feelings, and attitudes. Stress is pressure or other mental or physical reactions that people feel toward change. These **StressMatters** can leave you exhausted or energized depending upon how you approach change. This chapter will help you recognize how much stress you may have in your life. It also has suggestions for relieving stress in the future.

"After moving up from Mexico, I had trouble adjusting to different surroundings. Up here, lots of kids have called me dumb because I wasn't adjusting too good. If they had ever moved, they might understand that it's hard. I have some advice for someone who has moved. Try to get as many good friends as you can. The first friend might not be a good one. That might just be because you don't know what kind of friends you want. Keep on looking."

Change

Changes that cause stress such as divorce, unemployment, or lack of sleep can weaken the body's immune system. A weak immune system increases your chance of getting several infections and illnesses including heart diseases and cancer. A weak immune system also can delay the time wounds need to heal.

Dealing with life's changes can be difficult. You can't avoid them all. However, your attitude toward change makes a big difference. Positive or negative changes can alter your behavior, feelings, attitudes, and emotions.

Handling Change in Life

When teens talk about changes in their life, they often mention major events or tragedies. These big events and tragedies can have a tremendous effect. However, little changes can add up. Even enjoyable life-changing events may create as much stress as negative events.

Read through the following list of changes that can occur in a teen's life. On a sheet of paper, write down the number next to each event if it has happened to you in the last year. Events with a higher number cause more stress. Notice that the event with the highest amount of stress usually is considered a positive event.

Points	Event	Points	Event
101	Getting married	64	Having an unmarried teen sister become pregnant
92	Being pregnant and single		
87	Having a parent die	63	Being concerned about weight, height, or acne
81	Getting a visible physical defect	63	Having a parent get remarried
77	Becoming a single father	62	Having a visible physical defect since birth
77	Having parents divorce		
76	Getting involved with alcohol or other drugs	62	Experiencing a close friend's death
75	Having a parent put in jail for a year or more	58	Being seriously ill and hospitalized
69	Having parents separate	56	Failing a grade in school
68	Having a brother or sister die		
		56	Moving to a new school district
67	Experiencing a change in peers' acceptance of you	55	Having a parent become seriously ill
64	Discovering that you are adopted	55	Not making a team or other school activity
		53	Having a parent go to jail for 30 days or less

Change

Points	Event	Points	Event
53	Breaking up with a boyfriend or girlfriend	41	Having a brother or sister become seriously ill
51	Going on a first date	38	Having a parent be away from home more because of a new job
50	Getting a newborn sister or brother		
50	Being suspended from school	37	Having a brother or sister leave home
47	Arguing with parents more than before	36	Having a grandparent die
		34	Having a third adult added to the family
47	Having your physical appearance change because of braces or glasses	31	Becoming a fully committed member of a religion
46	Having a parent lose a job		
46	Having an outstanding personal achievement, such as winning a competition	31	Having a parent become pregnant
		27	Experiencing a decrease in parents' arguments
46	Seeing more arguments between parents	26	Having a mother begin to work outside the home
45	Having a parent make more or less money	26	Marriage of a sister or brother
43	Being accepted to attend a college you choose		

Add your points. The higher your score on this assessment, the higher your risk for physical and mental illness. It's unlikely that anyone will have the total of 2,432. A score of 150 or less is low risk. A score of 150–300 is medium risk. A score of over 300 is higher risk. If you or any of your friends scored over 300 points, be alert for any negative consequences from these changes.

WHAT DO YOU THINK?

Using the letters of your first name, look at the corresponding letters in the A to Z tips on pages 22 and 23. What changes do you need to make to follow the guidelines? Then do the same with the letters in your last name, and then the letters in the names of your relatives.

Change and Stress

Sometimes change threatens a person's physical, mental, emotional, or social health. Most teens face many changes. And most teens have great ability to deal with those changes. Some teens even flourish with change. They enjoy, get energized by, and are positively challenged by it. Learning to manage change is an important life skill.

On the other hand, change can be devastating. It may lead to uncontrollable stress and stress-related health problems. Such health problems may be biological or mental. Some biological problems include:

High blood pressure

Painful menstruation; menstruation is a monthly release of blood, fluid, and tissue in nonpregnant females

Sleep problems

Stomach illnesses

Migraine headaches

Skin rashes

Diarrhea, or condition in which normally solid body waste becomes loose and runny

Nausea and vomiting

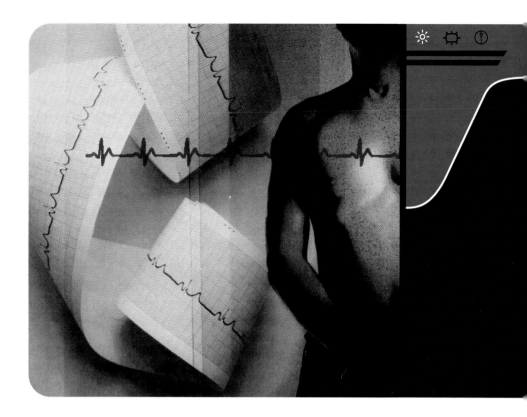

Some stress-related mental health problems include:

Fatigue

Depression

Irritability

Anger

As you've read, change can be positive and good. Unfortunately, it's not always that way. Some change hurts. It can cause sadness, pain, and loneliness. Change can cause a person to spiral into the depths of depression.

While we can't avoid change, there are many ways to cope with it. On the next page are some A to Z tips for handling changes and challenges.

A positive **attitude** can carry you past many problems.

Balance your day with work, fun, and being with other people.

Confidently accept and assert yourself every day.

Discover something new each day.

Escape mentally to a favorite place.

Flexibly adapt to change. Don't be stubborn when bad things happen.

Grow physically, mentally, emotionally, and socially. Practice the things you do well to get even better.

Find something **humorous** every day, in every situation.

Insulate yourself from people who want to infect you with negative thoughts, feelings, and attitudes.

Seek **joy** every day and do something fun.

Gain **knowledge** about yourself, others, and the world in which you live.

Listen to the voices within you. They are usually correct.

Remain **moral**, ethical, and trustworthy. Hold to your values.

Eat a **nutritious** diet that promotes growth and good health.

Organize your activities, events, responsibilities, and priorities. Priorities are the people, things, or ideas that you deal with first.

Prepare for change. Alter your preparations when necessary.

Get your **questions** answered. Reward yourself when you do.

Relax and unwind every day.

Seek, develop, and maintain relationships with other people. Join organized clubs, teams, and activities. Help others.

Talk with people of all ages and cultures. Talk to yourself in a positive way.

Use the wisdom that surrounds you.

Voice your thoughts on important issues.

Work out vigorously three times a week for at least 30 minutes. Walk when possible. Take the stairs instead of the elevator.

eXercise your brain, too. Challenge yourself with puzzles, games, problems, and memory activities.

Stay **young**. Play! Don't lose the child within you.

Get some **ZZZ's.** Give your mind and body the rest they need.

Points to Consider: StressMatters

Imagine that Juan has just moved from Mexico and joined your class. How could you help him adjust to that change?

Do you agree with the self-assessment that getting married is the most stressful event possible in a person's life? Why or why not?

Which of the A to Z tips do you think you are best at? Explain how this ability might help you handle change effectively.

Chapter Overview

Self-concept and self-esteem play a large part in how well people manage change. Many things can affect a person's self-esteem.

Each of us has two selves: the "actual self" and the "ideal self." The larger the gap between these selves, the lower a person's self-esteem is.

You can avoid some serious problems by learning more about your actual and ideal selves. A self-assessment can help you do that.

CHAPTER 3

Self-Esteem and Dealing With Change

In this chapter you will rate your self-esteem by finding the difference between your actual and ideal selves. These **PerceptionMatters** can have a major effect on how confidently you react to change.

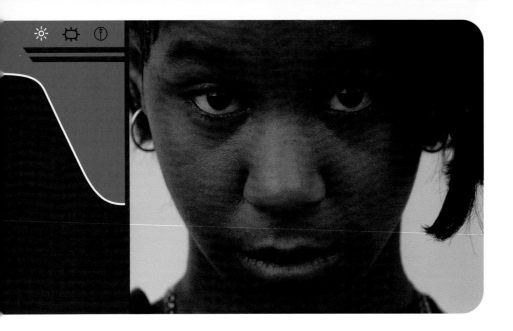

Angela is a senior in high school. She is doing great in school. She is on the honor roll, captain of the soccer team, and president of the student council. One day her mom came home and said that she was offered a job promotion. It would mean moving to another state, but she wanted to take it. Angela was stunned. She didn't want to leave her school and friends. However, she knew her mom really wanted the promotion. Angela didn't know what to do.

Self-Concept, Self-Esteem, and Change

Change occurs every day. Sometimes change is large, like the change Angela is facing. Sometimes it's small. Two things that help many people deal with large and small change are positive self-concept and self-esteem. They begin at birth and develop throughout life. They may be different every day, depending on many things.

"One big reason for teens' low self-esteem is the huge emphasis on looks and weight. You look in magazines and see those picture-perfect models and think, 'I'll never look that good.' Teens need to realize that those models have their hair styled and makeup put on by experts. Those pictures are fixed up so not one flaw is visible. This is not real! In life, there is more that counts than appearance, like personality and mind. Focus on those more than your looks, because they count so much more."—Trish, age 16

Self-Concept

Self-concept is a realistic understanding of your strengths and weaknesses. Your strengths include skills, abilities, expertise, talents, health, energy, and personality. Your weaknesses may be in emotional, social, or physical areas. They might include limitations, faults, and shortcomings.

Having a realistic self-concept can help you know which kinds of change you can manage. For example, imagine you are very energetic. If you lost one part-time job, you might find it easy to get out and look for another.

Self-Esteem

Along with your self-concept, self-esteem can help you deal with changes. Self-esteem is how much you value yourself and believe you are worth. The more you value yourself, the higher your self-esteem is.

Self-esteem plays a major role in how well you manage change. When you feel good about yourself you usually can deal with change better. Self-esteem is the basis of personality. People with positive self-esteem commonly feel good about themselves. They have a realistic view of their abilities and limitations.

Low self-esteem often is associated with serious health problems. These may include alcohol and other drug use, eating disorders, high-risk sexual behaviors, and suicide, or killing oneself.

The media can have a tremendous effect on our self-esteem. In books, magazines, movies, and ads, we often see perfect bodies and pretty people. Instead of inspiring us to look like that, these images often discourage us and lower our self-esteem.

Which of these people do you think has the highest self-esteem?

A star professional athlete

A famous movie actor

A successful medical doctor

A popular classmate in your school

A friendly salesperson in the mall

You

It could be you! Being rich or famous does not guarantee having high self-esteem.

Actual Self and Ideal Self

People with high self-esteem have little difference between their actual and ideal selves. Actual self is the person you really are. Ideal self is the person you would like to be. As the difference becomes greater between the actual and ideal perceptions, self-esteem lowers.

How is your self-esteem? Take the following self-assessment to find the difference between your actual and ideal selves.

Step 1   For each trait, write down the number that represents where you see yourself on the scale of 1–9. The lower numbers show that you believe the words on the left describe you best. The higher numbers show that you believe the words on the right are more accurate. This shows your actual self.

Step 2   Add any additional descriptive words and score them the same way.

Step 3   Then, next to the number showing your actual self, write down the number where you would like to be. This shows your ideal self.

Step 4   For each item, figure the difference between the two numbers. For example, say your actual self was 6 and your ideal self was 2 for the same description. The difference for that trait would be 6 – 2 = 4.

Step 5   Add up the differences for each of the traits. Lower totals indicate higher self-esteem. The lowest possible score is 0. Without any added items, the highest possible score is 176. If the gap between your actual self and ideal self is low, you probably have pretty good self-esteem. Areas in which the gap is higher are places you can improve.

outgoing	1	2	3	4	5	6	7	8	9	shy
calm	1	2	3	4	5	6	7	8	9	nervous
hard worker	1	2	3	4	5	6	7	8	9	loafer
kind	1	2	3	4	5	6	7	8	9	cruel
friendly	1	2	3	4	5	6	7	8	9	unfriendly
attractive	1	2	3	4	5	6	7	8	9	unattractive
energetic	1	2	3	4	5	6	7	8	9	sluggish
loving	1	2	3	4	5	6	7	8	9	unloving
active	1	2	3	4	5	6	7	8	9	inactive
cheerful	1	2	3	4	5	6	7	8	9	unhappy
wise	1	2	3	4	5	6	7	8	9	foolish
artistic	1	2	3	4	5	6	7	8	9	unartistic
musical	1	2	3	4	5	6	7	8	9	unmusical
athletic	1	2	3	4	5	6	7	8	9	unathletic
unselfish	1	2	3	4	5	6	7	8	9	selfish
confident	1	2	3	4	5	6	7	8	9	unconfident
spiritual	1	2	3	4	5	6	7	8	9	unspiritual
competent	1	2	3	4	5	6	7	8	9	incompetent
focused	1	2	3	4	5	6	7	8	9	unfocused
intelligent	1	2	3	4	5	6	7	8	9	unintelligent
leader	1	2	3	4	5	6	7	8	9	follower
important	1	2	3	4	5	6	7	8	9	unimportant

Change can come at us from all directions. It can sneak up on us without warning and surprise and startle us. Some change is unanticipated, or unexpected. Some change is predictable. The better your self-concept and self-esteem, the more successfully you probably can cope with change.

Points to Consider: PerceptionMatters

What advice would you give Angela about her mother's promotion? Why?

What is the difference between self-concept and self-esteem? Which is more important? Why?

Do you agree that being rich or famous doesn't automatically mean a person has high self-esteem? Why or why not?

How do you think you could close the gap between your actual and ideal selves?

Chapter Overview

Personality traits partly determine how people handle change.

Some of the traits that help people include self-efficacy, optimism, and sense of humor.

You can choose how you view change. Positive self-talk can be important in handling it.

Some experts describe two personality types, Type A or Type B. Most people's personality falls somewhere in between the types.

A self-assessment can help you see where your personality falls.

CHAPTER 4

✿

Personality

Personality has a big effect on how people view change. Your personality type might be impatient, easygoing, or something else. However, it probably is never all one way or another. In this chapter you will begin to identify how such **PersonalityMatters** can be strengths or weaknesses over which you have control.

In stressful situations, the mind and body prepare to respond to danger, either by fighting, running away, or doing nothing. This "fight, flight, or freeze" response includes a rapid heartbeat, cold or clammy hands and feet, upset stomach, and a feeling of dread. When the danger passes, the mind and body respond again. During this relaxation response, the heart slows down and the person experiences a sense of well-being.

Self-Efficacy and Coping With Change

Self-efficacy is the belief that you have the power and ability to accomplish a task. It's the belief that you are effective at what you do. If self-effective people believe they can stop smoking, start exercising, remain sexually abstinent, lose weight, or remain drug-free, chances are they can! If people believe they can't do these things, chances are their efforts will be hopeless.

Optimism and Dealing With Change

Optimistic people have a lot going for them. They tend to expect the best or dwell on the most hopeful aspects of a situation. Optimistic people usually expect a favorable outcome.

The opposite of an optimist is a pessimist. Pessimists tend to stress the negative or unfavorable or to take the gloomiest possible view. Optimistic people are often better able to cope with change than pessimists are.

Some researchers have found that students who scored high on tests about attitude reported fewer negative physical symptoms such as dizziness, fatigue, muscle soreness, and blurred vision. Optimism also is linked to faster and more successful recovery from surgery.

Optimism also has been linked scientifically to health. One way scientists measure people's immune system is by testing their saliva. This contains a substance call immunoglobulin A (IgA). Lower levels of IgA in a person's saliva are related to a weakened immune system. Thus, lower IgA levels are related to more frequent illness.

Scientists then studied the relationship between optimism and IgA levels. They found that the more optimistic a person is, the higher the IgA level. The more pessimistic, the lower the IgA level.

"People who laugh readily and view life with a sense of humor find change-causing stressful events less disturbing. Hearty laughter tones the heart and blood system, exercises the lungs, and releases muscular tension."
—David Meyers, professor of psychology

Sense of Humor and Handling Change

Have you ever heard the phrase "Laughter is the best medicine"? It seems to be literally true. When you are laughing, the brain is believed to release protective chemicals that boost the immune system. You can survive almost any change if a sense of humor is part of your personality. It can lighten many emotional loads and relieve the stress that life-changing events cause.

Some traits may have a basis in heredity. Some people believe they can't change things such as humorlessness, shyness, laziness, nervousness, or selfishness. Personal effort and desire can influence traits. So, don't automatically give up and just say, "That's my personality." Work on your sense of humor! You'll feel better.

Change: A Matter of Perception

Your attitude toward change is a powerful force. How you view the changes in your life may greatly alter the way the changes affect you.

Maryann and Christine, Ages 15 and 16

Maryann and Christine are 10th-grade students. After school today, both of them will try out for the school's track team. During the day, Maryann felt nervous and anxious. She told herself, "I don't think I can handle this." Her heart pounded, she ground her teeth, she felt tired, and her stomach was upset. She couldn't concentrate during math class. Maryann's interpretation of this life event caused a typically stress-related reaction in her.

Christine was nervous about the tryouts, too. However, she practiced coping with this life event. During her third-hour physical education class, she worked hard at her fitness routine. She knew that exercise is a stress reducer for her. Christine also relaxed, another way she knew she could reduce stress. She told herself, "I know I'm ready for this." And she focused on one aspect of the tryouts that made her feel good: The chance to be with friends.

Along with Type A and B, there's a new letter in the alphabet of personality types: Type H. People with Type H personality are constantly hostile. That is, they are angry, distrustful, and critical. More research on the Type H personality is being done.

You might think that you can't control your thoughts, but the fact is, you can! One way to do it is by your self-talk. Everyone talks to themselves. Some people say positive things to themselves, some say negative things. Positive self-talk can help you deal with change. Some people might say, "This is the worst thing in the world that could happen to me" or "I can't deal with this anymore." This may cause the change to linger and be more destructive.

Changing your thoughts and attitudes may not make the change less stressful. However, it may help you handle it better. You might say to yourself, "It could be worse," "Time will help me with this," or "I can hang in there." Try changing what you say to yourself about current or anticipated change. It can affect the way you respond to or cope with the change.

Evidence shows that Type A personality is associated with a slightly higher risk of coronary heart disease than Type B. Type A and Type B personalities are on opposite ends of the scale. Most people have some qualities of both Type A and Type B personalities.

Personality and Dealing With Change

Your personality can influence how well you deal with change. Some experts describe personality with the two terms Type A or Type B. Here are some words that describe each type. After reading the words, try the self-assessment on the next page.

Type A	Type B
Hardworking	Calm
Competitive	Relaxed
Impatient	Easy-going
Fast-talking	Poised
Fast-walking	Collected
Fast-eating	Gentle
Intense	Unruffled
Time pressured	Composed
Constantly rushing	

Read items 1–9 below. For each item, use a piece of paper to write the number that best describes your personality. Use this rating scale:

1 = Never   2 = Sometimes   3 = Always

1. I get impatient when I see someone working too slowly.	1	2	3
2. I feel I must win games rather than just have fun.	1	2	3
3. I find that there is never enough time.	1	2	3
4. I lose patience with people who are late.	1	2	3
5. I get impatient waiting for stop lights to turn from red to green.	1	2	3
6. I get frustrated when standing in a slow line.	1	2	3
7. I eat while getting dressed or working.	1	2	3
8. I finish sentences for people when they talk too slowly.	1	2	3
9. I make a fist when expressing my views or opinions.	1	2	3

What score did you get? Your score will be somewhere between 9 and 27 points. The closer your score is to 27 points, the more Type A characteristics you display. It's not necessarily bad, but you might want to work on relaxing a little.

Points to Consider: PersonalityMatters

The chapter mentions three things that influence how well a person copes with change. They are self-efficacy, optimism, and a sense of humor. Which of these do you notice most in your classmates? Why do you think this is true?

Do you think self-talk influences people's attitudes? Explain.

Do you see any advantages in having a Type A personality? a Type B personality? Explain.

Did you agree with your personality type identified in the self-assessment on page 42? Why or why not?

Chapter Overview

Loss and change that can't be controlled can cause depression.

Divorce and death are two types of uncontrollable change. Overwhelming emotions accompany them.

People can cope with death or help someone else cope, even though they can't control it.

CHAPTER 5

Uncontrollable Change and Loss

People may react to losses in their lives with sadness, hopelessness, anger, silence, or resistance. In this chapter you will become aware that some changes can create emotional nightmares. These might be called **HarshMatters.** You also will learn about positive, supportive ways to take care of yourself or others who experience loss.

Depression

Unexpected change can trigger feelings of emptiness and worthlessness in people. The line between feeling sad and becoming depressed is blurry. Sometimes sad feelings can lead to depression.

Everyone feels sad or blue at times. Sadness often follows changes in relationships with people. Arguments with family members and breakups with a boyfriend or girlfriend can bring on these feelings. Most teens can recover and bounce back from these temporary blues.

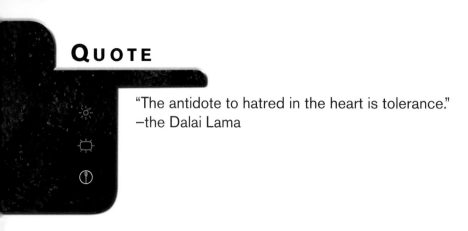
However, severe depression can occur when feelings of sadness, guilt, or hopelessness are exaggerated. This is true especially if these feelings continue over a long period of time. Sometimes the depression can be severe and cause overwhelming feelings of sadness and hopelessness. In these cases, suicidal thoughts may surface. To learn more about preventing depression and suicide, see Useful Addresses on page 61.

Divorce

One of the most traumatic changes for children or teens is their parents' divorce. Children of divorce are a diverse group. Some are wealthy, some are poor. They come from all backgrounds.

Children frequently are caught in nasty, even hostile, battles between the parents. The fight over who gets the child on holidays, weekends, and vacations can last for weeks. Some custody cases have lasted as long as 15 years and cost millions of dollars. Occasionally, one parent even kidnaps the child. The parents may try so hard to hurt each other that they neglect what's best for the child. Sometimes the child is asked to decide that one parent is good, the other bad.

Growing up in the middle of this conflict can be confusing and stressful for the child. Studies have been done of hundreds of children in situations where parents' arguments have continued for at least two years. These children have had difficulty forming stable relationships as adolescents and young adults.

Art, Age 19

"I grew up with a stay-at-home mother and an abusive, controlling father. At the divorce, I lied to the judge about my mother's faults. Dad had promised me a trip if I lied. I still feel guilty about it. My mother quit fighting the divorce when she ran out of money. Dad gained custody of me. My mother could visit me only two hours a month. Within a few years, she became a stranger. When I was older, I ran away to escape Dad. I haven't seen my mother for 10 years or my dad for 5 years.

Death

Death is a natural part of life. It's always around us. Many people first experience death through pets or other animals. Many teens know someone who has died. The death of a relative or close friend is sad and distressing. Understanding death often helps us better cope with the changes it brings.

DID YOU KNOW?

Victorian England had complicated rituals surrounding death. In the 1800s, most people died at home. The English prized the dying person's last words. Victorians discouraged the use of pain-relieving drugs so that the dying person could be conscious enough to speak.

Linda, Age 14

"When I was in sixth grade, my grandfather died. It only hit me at his funeral. Being with my family and seeing them crying made it worse. The next day in school I broke down and started to cry. My teachers comforted me while I waited for my mom to pick me up. I wasn't close to my grandfather. But it hurt that my teachers knew me better than my grandfather did.

"I don't know why I cried that day. Maybe it's that he was gone and it's too late to know him now. I've learned to deal with it though. I know that even though he never knew me, I was family, and that's what matters most."

All living things eventually die. Death can be defined in different ways. When does death occur? Years ago people often died of what was called "old age." They were considered dead when their heart and breathing stopped. Today, CPR or special medical equipment revive thousands of people whose heart or breathing stops. To deal with that fact, a careful definition of death has been developed. It still includes lack of breathing and heartbeat. But it also includes lack of physical reactions, reflexes, and brain activity.

"It is difficult to accept death in this society because it is unfamiliar. In spite of the fact that it happens all the time, we never see it."
—Elisabeth Kübler-Ross, psychiatrist

"It's not that I'm afraid to die, I just don't want to be there when it happens."
—Woody Allen, filmmaker

How to Handle Death

Dealing with loss through death requires time. There is no one right way to deal with this loss. People grieve and handle death differently. Parents who lose a child may grieve and cope differently from a child who loses a parent. Some people grieve and cope more publicly, others more privately.

Sometimes the kind of grief depends on whether the loss was sudden or anticipated. The grief resulting from unanticipated loss such as a car crash or murder is terrible. It may be different from that of an anticipated loss such as fatal illnesses. Yet, people have to deal with the loss. Sometimes a person grieves unnoticeably. The person may seem to have fully recovered from grieving when, in fact, the grieving continues. Often, people will cry unexpectedly. Special events and holidays are often especially difficult times.

The grieving person often experiences emotions such as sorrow, loneliness, guilt, or anger. The person may even feel relief. This can happen when the person who died was in severe pain.

These emotions can lead to physical problems. The problems may include difficulty sleeping, loss of appetite, and even a weakened immune system. This can lead to an increased likelihood of disease. Sometimes, loss through death places the survivor at greater risk of major illness, such as a heart attack.

Tips for Dealing With Death

Despite everything, it is possible to cope with death. Follow these guidelines, and you may handle someone's death better.

> Take care of yourself physically, mentally, emotionally, and socially. For example, eat well, exercise, and spend time with friends who care about you.
>
> Talk about the future. It will help offset the permanence of the death.
>
> Speak with people you can trust.
>
> Talk honestly about your feelings. Be open with yourself and others.
>
> Don't hide or run away from your feelings.
>
> Seek help when needed. Counseling is sometimes helpful when you can't get over the grief by yourself.

How to Help Someone Else Deal With Death

Many teens know friends or others who lose parents, brothers, sisters, and other loved ones. The death of a pet sometimes can be devastating for a young person. It's often difficult to know how to act and what to say. The best advice is to think of what you would like a friend to do if you were in this situation. Some guidelines include:

> Express your friendship, sympathy, and support. Don't be an absent friend.
>
> Listen to the person. Don't ask for the details of the death. The grieving person may or may not want to share them. Give the person time.

Reassure the person that emotions such as sadness, loneliness, and anger are normal.

Often hugging, holding, and touching tell the person you care.

Offer to put the grieving person in touch with others in similar situations. If you don't know others, then teachers, spiritual leaders, school counselors, or trained health professionals may.

Remember, everyone grieves differently in both time and responses. Don't be angry or impatient if the person grieves longer than you think is needed.

Points to Consider: HarshMatters

What's the difference between sadness and depression? Is it important? Why or why not?

What advice and assistance could you give to a teen whose parents are divorcing?

How could you help a friend or classmate whose loved one died?

If someone you loved had died, how would you want your friends to behave toward you?

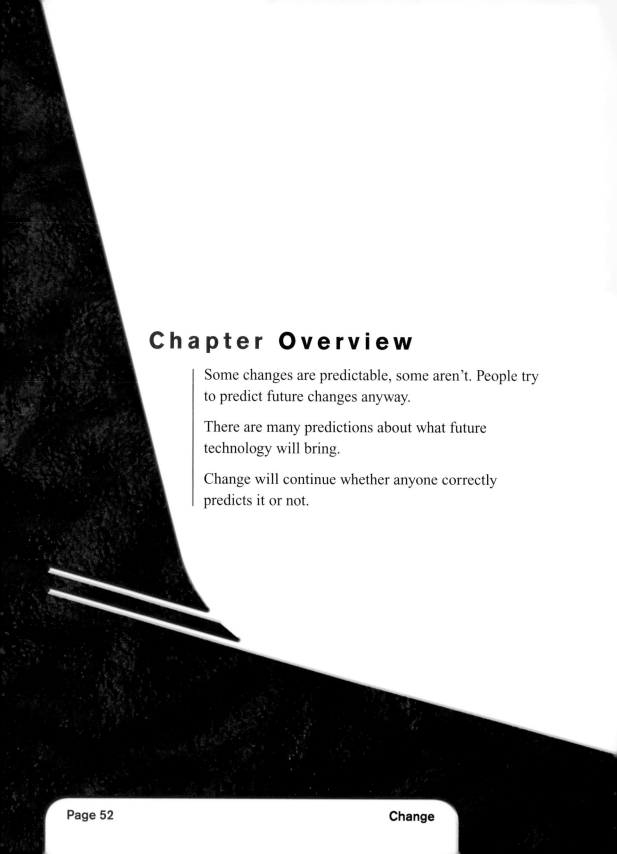

Chapter Overview

Some changes are predictable, some aren't. People try to predict future changes anyway.

There are many predictions about what future technology will bring.

Change will continue whether anyone correctly predicts it or not.

CHAPTER 6

☼

Change:
What's Ahead?

A hundred years ago, people didn't know that computers would create instant worldwide communication. People couldn't imagine freeze-dried food or medical advances that space travel made possible. In another hundred years, changes we can't imagine will cause lifestyles to be dramatically different from today. Change handled in a positive, healthy way can encourage creative thinking, imagination, and flexibility in preparing for the unexpected. In the future, **ImaginationMatters** will challenge your reality as well as your dreams.

When Ed's great-aunt couldn't live by herself anymore, she came to live with Ed and his family. "Gran," as Ed calls her, is 92 years old and has a sharp wit. Ed thinks it's funny that Gran rode a horse to school when she was his age. She didn't live in a house with electricity or indoor plumbing until she got married.

Ed can't believe that the world was ever that different. "How could you live without television or computers? What did you do for fun?" Ed asks her. Gran just laughs. "We played a lot of games," she says. "We read books. We told stories to each other. We put on plays for the family because we didn't have movies. People are still the same, Ed. You just have a lot more choices than I did."

Predicting Change

People can predict some changes in life. For example, children can expect a change in height, weight, and strength. Many people change homes or jobs. Most people can expect to meet new people and lose touch with old friends. Many people change their beliefs about some things as they gain new knowledge.

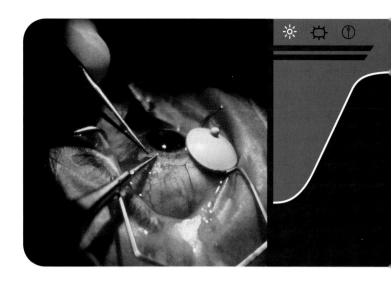

Some predictable changes happen at unpredictable times. For example, everyone dies. However, most people expect to die when they are old. It's possible for people to die unexpectedly at even a young age.

Some changes haven't yet taken place, but people try to predict them anyway. Many teens think about the future. They may set goals or dream about people they would like to meet or places they want to go. The predicted changes may include schools they would like to attend or a career or the family they want.

People living in the early 1900s never dreamed of:

- The Internet
- Microwave ovens
- Laser eye surgery
- Automobile air bags
- HIV infection and AIDS
- Leaf blowers
- Hand-held video games
- Nuclear warfare

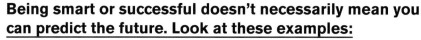

DID YOU KNOW?

Being smart or successful doesn't necessarily mean you can predict the future. Look at these examples:

"Heavier-than-air flying machines are impossible."
–William Thomson, British mathematician, 1895

"Drill for oil? You mean drill into the ground to try and find oil? You're crazy."–Drillers whom Edwin L. Drake asked to help him drill for oil in 1859

"Computers in the future may weigh no more than 1.5 tons."
–*Popular Mechanics* magazine, 1949

"Everything that can be invented has been invented."
–Charles H. Duell, Commissioner, U.S. Office of Patents, 1899

Some changes in our lives are a complete surprise. What changes do you think society will encounter during the next year, decade, or century?

A Look at the Future

Here are some predictions from technology scientists about what lies in the future.

Robots will clean our homes.

Household appliances will operate by voice commands. When you get up in the morning, you will just say to the lights, "Turn on" and to the furnace, "Warmer." In the kitchen, you will say to the toaster, "Make my toast." In an emergency you will say, "Get me an ambulance, the police, the fire department," and the sensors in the home will do it for you!

How about taking a space cruise that orbits the Earth and then staying in an orbiting hotel?

Want to have dinner with your relatives in a different state or country? A large, flat "techno" screen on the wall will arrange, organize, and schedule dinner with your relatives in real time.

Throw away your washing machine and ironing board. Many clothes will be made of "smart" fabrics that clean and press themselves.

Now that you've thrown away your washing machine, throw away your shower! Human washing machines will replace showers. These machines will automatically cycle you through soaping, washing, rinsing, and drying.

Electronic wallpaper will allow you to change the color and pattern of your walls with just the push of a button. You instantly can have any of your favorite paintings or posters electronically imaged on your wall.

You may never need keys again. Voice commands will open doors and start your car. Just say "open" or "start," and it will be done for you.

Cars and other vehicles will travel down magnetized highways at speeds of 100 to 200 miles per hour.

Machines that can scan your genetic structure (all 80,000 genes in your body) will inform you of symptoms or risks of disease.

Need a new body part? Just as we now replace worn-out parts in cars, replacing most worn-out or diseased body parts will become common.

The common cold? Don't get too optimistic. Although many diseases will be cured, the common cold isn't likely to be one of them.

Technology and the Future

Do these technological changes sound scary, intriguing, exciting, or even awesome? Time will tell to what degree, if any, they come true. As in the past, many technological changes will phase in, while older technologies phase out. New technologies are meant to make life easier, safer, and more efficient. For the most part you will grow and adapt to these changes.

In the years ahead, science and technology will decide what kind of change is possible. Be prepared. You and others may have the opportunity to decide which of these changes is appropriate and desirable.

Technology, however, will probably not be able to relieve you of the many social and interpersonal changes likely to occur during your lifetime. These are the change events that all of us must face from time to time. We will not have technology to help us, but we will have people to help us.

Friends will continue to move away. Parents will continue to get divorced. Loved ones will die. These changes can cause pain. They hurt. If we allow them, these changes can devastate our lives. As you grow older, you will face some changes and challenges that you never imagined.

With a positive attitude and a bit of practice you will be able to jump the many hurdles and changes that life puts in your way.

Enjoy the journey!

Points to Consider: ImaginationMatters

Give three examples of predictable and unpredictable life changes.

Name three things that have been invented in your lifetime. Have they changed your life for better or worse? Explain.

What changes in the future are you most excited about? Why?

What would you tell other teens to help them cope with the many life changes on the road ahead?

NOTE

At publication, all resources listed here were accurate and appropriate to the topics covered in this book. Addresses and phone numbers may change. When visiting Internet sites and links, use good judgment.

Internet Sites

Canadian Health Network
www.canadian-health-network.ca
Links to health topics

Go Ask Alice!
www.goaskalice.columbia.edu/index.html
Answers to questions about health-related issues including relationships, nutrition and diet, exercise, drugs, sex, alcohol, and stress

Last Acts: Care and Caring at the End of Life
www.lastacts.org
Promotes awareness of the need to improve care for the dying; includes electronic newsletter, searchable Resource Directory, and general information about the Last Acts Campaign

Hot Lines

Covenant House Nineline (24 hours a day)
1-800-999-9999

National Youth Crisis Hot Line
1-800-448-4663

Boys Town National Hot Line (Child Abuse)
13940 Gutowski Road
Boys Town, NE 68010
1-800-448-3000
1-800-448-1833 (TDD)

National Clearinghouse on Family Support and
Children's Mental Health
PO Box 751
Portland, OR 97207-0751
1-800-628-1696

National Foundation for Depressive Illness, Inc.
PO Box 2257
New York, NY 10116
1-800-239-1265
www.depression.org

National Institute of Mental Health
6001 Executive Boulevard
Room 8184
MSC 9663
Bethesda, MD 20892-9663
www.nimh.nih.gov

National Youth Crisis Hot Line
PO Box 178408
San Diego, CA 92177-8408

For Further Reading

Covey, Sean. *The Seven Habits of Highly Effective Teens.* New York: Simon and Schuster, 1998.

Doss, Bonnie, and Joyce Spindle. *But . . . What About Me! How It Feels to Be a Kid in Divorce.* San Antonio, TX: Bookmark Publishing, 1998.

Gregson, Susan R. *Stress Management.* Mankato, MN: Capstone, 2000.

Peacock, Judith. *Anger Management.* Mankato, MN: Capstone, 2000.

Glossary

actual self (AK-choo-wuhl SELF)—the person you really are, including your physical appearance, personality, family history, and emotional makeup

depression (di-PRESH-uhn)—overwhelming feeling of sadness that lasts a long time

ideal self (eye-DEE-uhl SELF)—the person you wish to be

life-change events (LIFE-CHANJ ee-VENTSS)—little events that occur on a regular basis or major events, including celebrations and tragedies, that affect or change your life

optimistic (op-tuh-MISS-tik)—hopeful, cheerful, and confident

perception (pur-SEP-shuhn)—awareness that you have about yourself or others

pessimistic (pess-uh-MISS-tik)—gloomy, negative

positive self-talk (POZ-uh-tiv SELF-tok)—encouraging yourself that what you are doing is right, helpful, or important

priorities (prye-OR-uh-teez)—the people, things, or ideas that get your first thoughts or considerations

self-efficacy (self-EF-uh-kuh-see)—belief in yourself and your power to create positive change

stress (STRESS)—pressure, strain, or a mental reaction caused by positive or negative change

unanticipated change (uhn-an-TISS-uh-pay-tuhd CHANJ)—unexpected change, which can be small or big, positive or negative

Index

activities, 12, 19, 22
actual self, 25, 29, 30
alcohol, 12, 18, 28
Amish, 9
appearance, 18, 19, 27, 31
attitudes, 7, 11, 15, 17, 22, 37, 38, 40, 59

babies, 10, 19
balance, 22
behavior, 15, 17, 28
breaking up, 19, 45

car crashes, 6, 49
challenge, 20, 53, 59
change, 5–12, 20, 21, 22, 23, 26, 35, 40, 45, 53–55, 57, 59. *See also* mental reactions; physical reactions
    adapting to/coping with, 12, 32, 36, 37, 38, 39, 47, 58
    effects of, 17, 20, 21, 38
    handling, 11, 17, 38, 40, 41, 53
    managing, 20, 27
    negative, 7–9, 10, 11, 17
    positive, 6, 7–8, 10, 11, 17, 18, 20, 21
    predicting, 54–58
    resisting, 9, 45
    uncontrollable, 45
ChangeMatters, 5
college, 19
communication, 6. *See also* talking
communications, 9. *See also* telephones
confidence, 7, 22, 25, 31

dating, 19
death, 6, 18, 47–51, 55
defects, 18
diet, 12, 22
divorce, 8, 9, 17, 18, 46–47
drugs, 12, 18, 28, 36

eating patterns, 28, 41, 49, 50
emotions, 5, 12, 17, 20, 38, 45, 49, 50. *See also* feelings
events, 5, 17, 18–19, 22, 38, 39, 49
exercise, 12, 23, 36, 39, 50

family, 18, 19, 45, 46, 47, 50, 55, 57
fatigue, 21, 37
feelings, 6, 7, 15, 17, 50
    anger, 21, 45, 49, 51
    anxious, 39
    depression, 21, 45–46
    guilt, 46, 47, 49
    irritability, 21
    loneliness, 21, 49, 51
    nervous, 9, 39
    sadness, 21, 45–46, 47, 51
    scared, 9, 58
fighting, 9, 19, 45, 46
flexibility, 22, 53
friends, 9, 16, 18, 26, 39, 47, 50, 54
future, 7, 15, 50, 53, 55, 56–57

goals, 7, 12, 55
grieving, 48, 49, 50, 51
growth, 6, 8, 22, 54